THE NATIONAL AUDUBON SOCIETY COLLECTION
NATURE SERIES

NORTH AMERICAN
BIRDS

THE NATIONAL AUDUBON SOCIETY COLLECTION
NATURE SERIES ™

NORTH AMERICAN
BIRDS

Text by Barbara Burn

Foreword by Christine Sheppard, Associate Curator of Ornithology,
The New York Zoological Society

Bonanza Books • New York

All of the photographs in this book are from Photo Researchers/National Audubon Society Collection. The name of the individual photographer follows each caption.

Photographers' credits for uncaptioned photographs in the front and back matter of this book are (in order of appearance): Jeanne White, Stephen Collins, O. S. Pettingill, Jr., Calvin Larsen, Pat and Tom Leeson, Jim Zipp, Calvin Larsen, Townsend P. Dickinson, Tom and Pat Leeson, Harry Engels, Charlie Ott, and Rod Planck.

I would like to express my deep appreciation to Chris Sheppard of the New York Zoological Society (The Bronx Zoo) for her careful reading of the manuscript and for her many helpful suggestions. Any errors that may appear in this book, however, are entirely my own.
—*Barbara Burn*

The National Audubon Society Collection Nature Series
Staff for this book
General Editor: Robin Corey
Photo Researcher: Nancy Golden
Production Editor: Jean T. Davis
Designer: June Marie Bennett
Production Manager: Laura Torrecilla
Production Supervisor: Cindy Lake

This 1984 edition is published by Bonanza Books, distributed by Crown Publishers, Inc., 225 Park Avenue South, New York, New York 10003
THE NATIONAL AUDUBON SOCIETY COLLECTION NATURE SERIES is a trademark owned by the National Audubon Society, Inc.

Manufactured in Italy

Library of Congress Cataloging in Publication Data

Burn, Barbara.
North American birds.
(The National Audubon Society collection nature series)
Includes index.
1. Birds—North America.   I. Title.   II. Series.
QL681.B83   1984   598.297   83-24311

ISBN: 0-517-44741X

h g f e d c b

THE NATIONAL AUDUBON SOCIETY AND ITS MISSION

In the late 1800s, forward-thinking people became concerned over the slaughter of plumed birds for the millinery trade. They gathered together in groups to protest, calling themselves Audubon societies after the famous painter and naturalist John James Audubon. In 1905, thirty-five state Audubon groups incorporated as the National Association of Audubon Societies for the Protection of Wild Birds and Animals, since shortened to National Audubon Society. Now, with more than half a million members, five hundred chapters, ten regional offices, a twenty-five million dollar budget, and a staff of two hundred seventy-three, the Audubon Society is a powerful force for conservation research, education, and action.

The Society's headquarters are in New York City; the legislative branch works out of an office on Capitol Hill in Washington, D.C. Ecology camps, environmental education centers, research stations, and eighty sanctuaries are strategically located around the country. The Society publishes a prize-winning magazine. *Audubon:* an ornithological journal, *American Birds:* a newspaper of environmental issues and Society activities, *Audubon Action:* and a newsletter as part of the youth education program, *Audubon Adventures.*

The Society's mission is expressed by the Audubon Cause: to conserve plants and animals and their habitats, to further the wise use of land and water, to promote rational energy strategies, to protect life from pollution, and to seek solutions to global environmental problems.

National Audubon Society 950 Third Avenue New York, New York 10022

CONTENTS

FOREWORD

Long ago, men and birds lived in balance. *Homo sapiens* was just one more predatory participant in the food chain, anxious to catch and eat any available protein and anxious to avoid becoming potential food for vultures. Man was in close contact with his environment, attuned to any signals that could affect his survival such as the movements and behavior of birds. These signals were important for timing the seasons, warning of danger, predicting weather, and finding food. Strange and wonderful to land-bound man, birds were thought to have mystical powers, and myths arose as human culture developed—about the eagle's strength, the owl's wisdom, the happy song of the lark.

Then settlements began to change the face of the land and, over the centuries, only a few species of birds could use these changes to their advantage. Most retreated—into the forests, to the mountains, to areas not yet colonized by man.

Throughout history there have always been a few naturalists studying the complexities and secrets of living birds, yet, to the majority of people, birds were a source of food, whether raised in domestic flocks or hunted in the wild. Increasing human population coupled with the development of the shotgun and other efficient weapons in the early twentieth century turned hunting to slaughter. Killing of wild birds for market, for sport, or for no reason at all reached such proportions that the passenger pigeon, a species that once numbered in the billions, was exterminated within a few decades.

Simultaneously, increased technology produced leisure time for many people. Freed from six-day work weeks and twelve-hour work days, individuals had time to look around: many people, including some recreational hunters, were dismayed to note the rate at which both songbirds and gamebirds were disappearing. As a result, the number of people interested in birds and in their conservation has steadily increased. Overhunting in the United States has been largely controlled through legislation. The latter half of the twentieth century, however, has seen a new series of crises for birds and humans as we struggle with the consequences of industrial development. Pesticides, habitat degradation, and water pollution all have adverse effects on all kinds of life. Because birds are so sensitive to these changes, they are now studied as indicators of the general health of our planet.

Many people are concerned about declining populations of birds not because they are an early warning system for human populations but because birds themselves are so fascinating. A bird's body and behavior are designed around the fact of flight. The ability to fly has as many restrictions as privileges, and it affects everything from reproduction (birds lay eggs because they cannot fly well while carrying embryos) to feeding (swallows feeding on a swarm of bees in the air are skillful enough to select only stingless drones). Even a backyard bird feeder can become a source of bird lore, as species set up hierarchies for access to food or bring their young to the feeder in spring. Most species, however, do not live in close association with human populations in urban and suburban areas. It is worth the small effort to get out and see a flock of geese on a nearby pond or to wake a little earlier than usual to watch for migratory warblers.

Many of us have lost touch with the fact that we, too, are animals, dependent on interactions with our environment. It is too easy to ignore our own biology nowadays. The most important and astonishing thing for us to observe in birds is not their difference from us humans but their similarities. Man is often arrogant about being unique in the animal kingdom. The lesson of birds lies in showing us the ways in which we are not unique. The problems of life are universal.

CHRISTINE SHEPPARD
Associate Curator of Ornithology
1984   The New York Zoological Society

NORTH AMERICAN
BIRDS

INTRODUCTION

Nature is immensely complex, involving millions of different species of animals and plants that are connected to one another through complicated interrelationships and that live by certain laws even scientists do not fully understand. Yet because we humans are also part of that intricate web of nature, the study of natural history is one that appeals to all of us, though we may have little interest in hiking miles into wilderness areas to witness the wonders of nature at first hand. Fortunately, it is not necessary to spend a great deal of time and effort to learn about the natural world; in fact, one need go no further than the backyard or the local city park to observe wildlife. Although few of us will ever hold a wild bird in our hands or be capable of

The Baltimore oriole (left) and the western meadowlark (above) are closely related species in the passerine order of birds, the largest order in the world and, many scientists believe, the most recently evolved.
(Bill Dyer, left; Anthony Mercieca, above)

recognizing more than a few dozen species, it is possible for even the most amateur of naturalists to comprehend the basic principles of our environment by watching birds in action.

Bird-watching is certainly one of the most popular of our national pastimes, partly because it is fun to track down or "hunt" for different species in their natural habitat and partly because birds are the most accessible form of wildlife—they are colorful, noisy, and easy to see. Since they are sensitive to the world around them, birds can tell us much about the quality of the environment we live in. It was Rachel Carson's book *The Silent Spring,* sadly predicting the disappearance of birdsong, that made Americans aware of the dangers of pesticides—not only to the insects they were designed to kill but also to birds, other animals, and humans as well. Where birds are numerous and varied, one can be sure that the quality of water, air, and earth are high

11

enough to support life on many different levels.

There are nearly nine thousand species of birds in the world, of which almost seven hundred are native to North America, either as year-round residents or as visitors on their regular migrations. These species represent twenty orders—major groups of birds that share certain characteristics of body structure and appearance. These orders are ranked by scientists according to their evolutionary development, from the most primitive or oldest order, Gaviiformes, which includes the loons, to the most recently evolved order, the Passeriformes or perching birds, which includes hundreds of species of songbirds such as the warblers, thrushes, and finches. Each order comprises one or more families, of which there are seventy-eight in North America, and nearly all of them are represented in this book. Because there are so many species within most families, however, we cannot discuss them all here, although they are included in several excellent field or identification guides listed in the Suggested Reading section at the back of the book.

The intention of this book is to introduce the reader to the wide range of our native wild birds, using representative species to show how varied, adaptable, and fascinating these creatures are. Since many kinds of birds live in each different North American habitat—from the seashores and the forests to the deserts and the highest mountains—we will look at certain birds according to the areas in which they can be found at least part of the year.

The North American continent is divided by scientists into five major types of environments: tundra, coniferous (or evergreen) forests, deciduous forests, grasslands, and desert. Some of these areas have changed greatly over the last few hundred years because of the increase in human population, which has radically altered the landscape. Huge cities were built where marshes and shorelines once existed, inhabited only by wild animals. And forests have been eliminated to create farmlands and meadows. Nevertheless, many birds—especially those introduced here from other parts of the world by humans—have been able to adapt themselves to the new environments and can still be found throughout the land. Birds have always been

adaptable. Scientists believe that the first birds actually descended from reptiles in the age of the dinosaurs, developing feathers from scales and making other adjustments in their bodies—warm-bloodedness, minimal bone structure, and other special adaptations such as bills, wings, and claws—that enabled them to fly and find food. It is estimated that most North American bird families evolved between 28 million and 10 million years ago and that most of the species we know today have existed on the continent for at least a million years.

In spite of the incredible variety in birds, there are a number of characteristics that all birds share, the most obvious one being the possession of feathers, which no other animals have. (Bats, which are mammals, can fly, of course, and so can insects, and reptiles, together with a few mammals, can lay eggs, but feathers are truly unique to birds.) Feathers are important to flight, but they do not exist only on wings; feathers serve as insulation to protect delicate skin, to retain warmth, and to keep water away from

The brilliantly colored male cardinal is easily recognized by its plumage. As in many other species, the female is much duller in color. (Helen Williams)

Wild turkeys may eat soft foods, such as insects and berries, but seeds, nuts, and acorns are an important part of their diet. These foods are difficult to digest, but turkeys are equipped with well-developed gizzards to grind them up.
(Stephen J. Krasemann)

the body. Their colors and patterns provide protective camouflage for some species and are a means of identification among others. Small birds usually have fewer than 5,000 feathers, while water birds—which require greater insulation—can have as many as 10,000 to 12,000. Only fifty or so of these feathers are actually used in flying; a flying bird might have ten or twelve primary feathers at the tip of each wing with six or seven secondary feathers beneath them and twelve or more feathers in the tail.

As feathers become worn, they are replaced by new ones on a regular basis in a process called molting. Some species of birds molt a few feathers at a time, taking a whole year to replace their plumage, while others molt in just a few weeks, usually when they are not busy migrating, laying eggs, or raising babies. The offspring of many species are born without any feathers at all and grow down feathers and often a second, or juvenile, plumage before acquiring their adult feathers. Other species of birds are born with a full

covering of down, but they too often do not begin to resemble adults in appearance until they are sexually mature and ready for breeding.

Although some birds, such as ostriches and penguins, do not fly, most people connect birds with the idea of flight. As one can easily see when watching birds in the air, they do not all fly in the same way. Hummingbirds hover in the air—beating their wings up to sixty times a second just to stay in place—while hawks and other birds of prey soar on wind currents and "thermals" (columns of rising warm air) to save their energy during their long hours in flight. Some birds, such as quails, can spring up into the air and fly for short distances, while others are strong, streamlined fliers efficiently built to fly against the wind and to flap their wings for long periods of time. Some tiny songbirds can maintain speeds of 20 miles per hour for quite a distance, while a few expert fliers, such as swifts and falcons, have been clocked at more than 150 miles per hour.

Snow geese, shown here in flight and feeding, can tolerate the extreme conditions of the Arctic tundra, where they nest in summer in large colonies, with as many as twelve hundred pairs in one square mile. (Calvin Larsen)

Another special characteristic of birds is the bill, which enables them to collect or capture food. Birds use up a great deal of energy and must eat often; most of their time, in fact, seems to be taken up in searching for food and then in catching it. For this reason, their eyesight is exceptionally good and most birds are able to see colors, unlike most mammals. Although many species are relatively specialized in the kind of food they eat, birds in general can eat almost anything—plants (including seeds, fruits, nuts, leaves, buds, and sap) and animals (insects, worms, crustaceans, fish, reptiles, amphibians, other birds, and mammals), which means that they are active at all levels of the food chain. The bill shape often indicates what sort of feeder a bird is: Long curved bills are good for probing into trees or underneath the ground or water, while short straight bills pick food off surfaces; hooked bills can tear flesh, while short, thick bills can crush seeds. Feet, too, differ from one species to another, depending on the way a bird moves and

captures its food: Swimming birds have webbed feet to help them move through the water, while wading birds have long toes to help keep them stable on mud flats; birds of prey have sharp talons to help them kill and carry their food.

Birds do not have teeth to enable them to break down their food before they swallow, nor can they afford to carry the extra weight of undigested food as they fly, so their digestive systems are simpler and different from ours. A bird's stomach has two compartments, one that excretes gastric juices to digest soft food, such as insects and fruits, and the other, a muscular gizzard, that crushes food. Some species swallow sand or gravel which remains in the gizzard to help it grind up hard food, such as seeds. Many birds have a crop, an enlargement of the esophagus in the neck that enables them to store food before it is digested; in some species, such as domestic chickens, food is broken down chemically in the crop, and in others, such as grouse, the crop produces a loud sound during courtship. All birds need water, and many take it in the food they eat rather than drinking it; seabirds and those that live in brackish water near the sea have special glands that enable them to filter out the salt.

Bird ears, which are covered with feathers, are not visible, and yet we know that they can hear well because of the wide variety of noises that birds make—mostly in communicating with each other. The hobby of bird-watching, indeed, could better be called "bird-listening," since most species can be accurately identified by the sounds they produce. Not all bird noises are songs; ornithologists use the term "songs" for vocalizations directed at rivals or mates. They use the term "calls" for other messages, such as warning or alarm sounds.

In most songbird species, only the male sings, since he is often responsible for setting up the nesting territory and keeping other males away while he attracts a suitable female for himself—all of which he does while singing a distinctive pattern of notes. This is why most birdsong is heard only at certain times of year—when birds are active in the beginning of the breeding season—and at certain times of day—early morning and late afternoon, when activity is greatest, though some birds prefer to sing at night (the mockingbird and the whip-poor-will are well-known night singers). Songs vary according to the place where a bird lives: Birds on or close to the ground must use lower-pitched sounds that will travel far, whereas birds living in the tops of trees usually produce high-pitched songs.

Unlike songs, calls can occur at any time of year, when birds wish to communicate danger or aggression or simply to inform others where they are, as in migration or when raising their young.

Scientists have discovered that while most bird vocalizations are innate, many birds learn their own species' songs and calls by imitating. This still does not explain, however, why some birds, such as mockingbirds and parrots, have developed the ability to mimic the noises of species other than their own. Crows, jays, and starlings are also good mimics, and some can even be taught to "speak" human language, although they do not understand what they are saying.

Aside from finding food and avoiding enemies, the most persistent form of activity in birds is nesting, which varies enormously from one species to the next. Nevertheless, there are certain basic features in bird reproduction. In all species, the male and female must join together to fertilize the eggs within the female; eggs must be laid and incubated until they hatch in some safe, warm place, usually a nest, and the young birds must be fed and protected until they can fend for themselves.

Many species move from their winter quarters, usually in warm climates, to a regular breeding area in the spring, when they begin the annual business of finding a nesting territory, joining their mates, building or finding a nest, and defending it against other birds. The purpose of these nesting territories is complex, but one important reason is to enable each pair to raise its family without competing for food with their own kind. Some birds are colonial nesters, breeding in huge groups with only a few inches to themselves, while others—such as some birds of prey—need huge territories of several square miles.

Breeding activity itself is fascinating in its wide variety from one species to another, involving not only songs but also beautiful plumage and elaborate courtship displays that include special dances, flight patterns, and feeding behavior, depending on the species. After breeding, the males of some species may depart, leaving the female to incubate the eggs and raise the young by herself, but most baby birds require so much food that many parents share chick-rearing responsibilities.

Nests can be elaborate woven constructions or simple holes in the ground or in trees, lined only with grasses or feathers, but most birds make some place for the eggs to be laid and hatched in safety.

The shape and coloration of the egg are often remarkably appropriate to a nest's location. Birds nesting on cliffs, for instance, usually lay eggs that are pointed at one end and thus are less likely to roll off the edge, while birds with secure nests lay nearly round eggs; ground-nesting birds usually lay eggs that are well camouflaged against the ground, while tree-nesters often lay pale-blue or green eggs that are less visible in dappled light. Eggs laid in tree holes are often white, making it easy for the parents to locate them in the

Young robins are relatively helpless after hatching and must be fed by the adult; they are ready to fly, however, after only two weeks. (Arthur C. Twomey)

A California condor chick may be fed by its parents for more than a year. The slow reproduction rate of this extremely rare bird means that its population may not be able to increase sufficiently to ensure the species' survival. (Tom McHugh)

dark; presumably the nest site is safe enough from predators that camouflage is not necessary.

The number of eggs in a clutch, the number of clutches in a season, and the number of days it takes for eggs to hatch vary greatly from one species to the next and usually seem to be adjusted to the bird's environment. In most cases, incubation does not begin until nearly all of the eggs in a clutch are laid, so that the chicks will hatch at about the same time. The period of time for incubation usually depends on whether the chicks are altricial (helpless and often naked at birth) or precocial (usually covered with down and ready to leave the nest to swim or walk within a few hours); the latter, of course, spend more time developing in the egg than the former. The amount of time the parents spend feeding their young also varies—bald eaglets may stay in the nest for eight weeks or more, but Canada goslings feed themselves, under parental supervision, shortly after hatching.

Raising baby birds is undoubtedly one of nature's most exhausting occupations, requiring a constant search for food and endless trips back to the nest. Once the nestlings have lost their down and grown their first flight feathers, they become known as fledglings and within a short time are capable of going off on their own, eventually to join the adult world in the age-old pattern of breeding and raising young.

Like flight, migration is a dramatic aspect of bird behavior. Ornithologists agree that the principal reason for migration—moving from winter quarters in spring to nesting grounds and then back in the fall—has to do with the availability of food and the longer northern days in which to feed offspring. It is theorized that the coming of glaciers in the Ice Age forced birds living in the North to migrate south to warmer areas; certainly it is cold weather as well as the shortened day that triggers the migratory urge in the fall, and we know that mild weather and an abundance of food may cause some migrating birds to cease or shorten their travels. Some birds travel immense distances, usually in a north-south direction, while others traditionally move only a few hundred miles; a few species, called residents, fail to migrate at all.

Studies of banded ducks and other game birds seem to indicate that many species return to the same nesting areas year after year. How they find their way is not fully understood, but it is assumed that most birds orient themselves by the position of the sun and stars. Day travelers undoubtedly use landmarks to guide them, and some scientists believe that the earth's magnetic field also plays an important part in determining a bird's direction. Whatever the true answer, the sight of hundreds of birds flying in formation or in vast flocks is a spectacular one, and the annual return of the cliff swallows to Capistrano in Southern California on or around March 19 every year is a mystery at which we can only wonder.

Now that we have briefly touched on some of the fascinating characteristics shared by nearly all birds, let's take a closer look at some of the wonderful ways in which different species vary. As we shall see, many birds live in similar habitats but within them lead very different lives. Some of the birds we will meet in the pages that follow may never meet one another on the same shore or in the same forest, since they inhabit different parts of the continent, but they have developed similar traits to cope with the common problems of feeding and nesting in similar types of environment.

Golden eagles, native to the mountain ranges of North America, may have an exclusive territory as large as fifty square miles. (Tom Myers)

BIRDS OF THE SEA

Although this skua looks peaceful enough on the beach, it is actually a bird of prey, stealing fish from other birds and attacking ducks and gulls. (George Holton; see page 26.)

The oceans of the world are vast, covering more than two-thirds of the earth's surface, and it is not surprising that many bird species spend some of their time in the airspace over the sea, traveling along their migratory routes to and from their nesting grounds. A few species, however, derive their entire livelihood from the ocean, feeding offshore or far out at sea on fish, plankton, or crustaceans. All of them come to land to nest, but the true pelagic or oceanic birds—such as the albatrosses, shearwaters, petrels, and storm-petrels—fly over the oceans for most of the year without ever touching the earth. In this chapter, we will meet these marathon fliers, along with some coastal species that feed at sea rather than along the shore.

It is interesting to note that many of these birds share similar characteristics: They are excellent fish catchers with good eyesight and specially formed bills; they are superb fliers, usually with long, slender wings of great strength; they are long-lived, up to twenty years or more; and they are largely white in color. The reasons for this coloration are not fully understood, but ornithologists believe it relates to their feeding habits; since the ocean provides an ample amount of fish for these birds, they will often feed in groups, and when one bird discovers a school of fish from the air, its white color serves to alert other birds and attract them to the spot, as well as being less visible against the sky when seen from below. The few seabirds that are not white generally feed in different ways, swimming on the surface or close to it, so for them visibility is not an important factor.

Another interesting trait shared by seabirds is their ability to drink salt water. Like humans, birds must limit the amount of salt in their bodies to less than 1 percent of body

This gannet pair is performing its courtship display among hundreds of other gannets, for these members of the booby family often breed in vast colonies. (B. Griffeths; see page 24.)

fluids, for the kidneys are incapable of excreting excess salt indefinitely without dehydrating the body and causing eventual death. It was not until the 1950s that scientists discovered a special pair of nasal salt glands in seabirds, which enable the birds to eliminate salt from seawater before it is ingested. The ancient mariner's "Water, water, every where, nor any drop to drink" would have made little sense to the birds that he saw flying over the ocean around him.

BLACK-FOOTED ALBATROSS

The bird that the ancient mariner probably saw was the wandering albatross, the largest and most spectacular of all oceanic birds. There are thirteen species of albatross worldwide, but only seven are seen off the North American coasts. The black-footed albatross occurs off the Pacific coast, often following ships and feeding on garbage, although its primary diet is fish and squid. These birds nest in Hawaii, but they range over the entire North Pacific and like other albatrosses are capable of spending months over the ocean, landing only occasionally on the surface to feed. They are magnificent fliers, gliding for miles on prevailing wind currents, but their wings are not designed for efficiency in flapping or in taking off from the ground. To launch themselves into the air, albatrosses either run along the ground or drop off a cliff onto an air current. Their short, webbed feet cause them to be ungainly on land, but they are extremely graceful in courtship, performing wonderful ritualized displays. Pairs are believed to mate for life. In the nineteenth century, albatrosses were hunted for their feathers; this later led Theodore Roosevelt to set aside some nesting areas as protected reserves in 1909.

SOOTY SHEARWATER

Members of the shearwater family, which includes fulmars and petrels, are commonly called tubenoses because of the shape of their nostrils. They appear to have a highly developed sense of smell, which draws them to fish-oil odors from miles away. Like the albatrosses, to which they are related, shearwaters are gliding birds with long, narrow wings, and they spend most of their year at sea feeding on fish and crustaceans, coming ashore only to breed. Their name comes from their manner of flying low over the water between waves, for they seem to shear the tips of the waves with their wings; occasionally they will dive and fish underwater as well. Sooty shearwaters nest between November

The albatross, like most seabirds, is a brilliant flier that spends most of the year at sea. On land it is a relatively awkward bird, although the albatross pair, which mates for life, performs an elegant courtship display at the beginning of each nesting season. (Gilbert S. Grant)

and March on islands in the southern hemisphere, off South America, New Zealand, and Australia, and can be seen off both Atlantic and Pacific coasts in the summer months, often flying and feeding in enormous flocks. The shearwaters make the longest migrations of all southern hemisphere breeders and can be found as far north as Labrador and Greenland in late summer.

WILSON'S STORM-PETREL

Closely related to the shearwaters, the storm-petrel family includes the smallest of the seabirds; they are about the size of a robin and are known to sailors as Mother Carey's chickens, since they are often seen in flocks and when nesting make constant chirping sounds. Because they often appear during windy weather, their presence seems to herald the arrival of a storm, hence the name storm-petrel. They, too, are gliders and when feeding fly very close to the surface. The Wilson's storm-petrel (named for ornithologist Alexander Wilson), which is seen more often off the Atlantic coast than the Pacific, is believed to be the most abundant bird in the world. Like the sooty shearwater, it breeds in the southern hemisphere and migrates annually as far as the Arctic, often following the Gulf Stream, where it is a very common sight as it follows fishing boats for scraps. It feeds primarily on plankton, but it also feeds on small fish and crustaceans.

BROWN PELICAN

This bird is a familiar sight along the North Atlantic coast, mostly in the southeast, and also on the west coast, but it is not a true oceanic bird, since it spends much of its time near or on the land. Nevertheless, the brown pelican feeds almost exclusively on saltwater fish (unlike the other North American pelican, the white, which is found mainly on freshwater lakes), diving from the air—sometimes from a height of sixty feet or more—when it sights fish in the water below. To aid them in fishing, pelicans have two very special pieces of equipment: their remarkable bill, which supports a skin pouch that squeezes the water out of the mouth before swallowing (they do not carry fish in the pouch), and air sacs under their skin to cushion the impact of landing on water and to bring them quickly back to the

The sooty shearwater is generally seen in flocks at sea, skimming over the waves. This is an unusual close-up shot. (Barbara Peterson)

Wilson's storm-petrel is one of the most numerous birds in the world. It travels many miles at sea each year on its migratory routes. (Bill Wilson)

surface. Pelicans are the largest water birds, weighing as much as fifteen pounds with a wingspread of six to nine feet, and like the albatrosses are awkward on land but graceful in the air, soaring like eagles, often to great heights. Pelicans are very gregarious, living in flocks, and were once much more common than they are today. Because they feed on coastal fishes that are subject to heavy pollution, they have declined drastically in numbers during this century. The use of pesticides that cause eggshells to become so thin that they cannot be incubated has been controlled in some areas, however, and pelican populations are beginning to make a strong comeback or at least to remain stable.

GANNET

Like the pelican, the gannet dives for fish from great heights and has similar air sacs in its body to soften the blow of landing on water. It is a member of the booby fam-

ily, the only one to nest in North America; it can be found on cliffs and islands off the coast of Canada in the North Atlantic. All of the birds in this family are goose-sized with webbed feet and long pointed wings, and though they are seen mostly in coastal waters, they spend much of their time out at sea, especially during their first three years before they become breeding adults. Like the other boobies, gannets are colonial nesters, grouping together in flocks of several hundred or more and often occupying the same nesting sites year after year. The name "booby" comes from the Spanish word for "dunce," probably because these birds are fearless and easy to catch; they are protected by law but the reason for their survival is undoubtedly that their nesting areas are relatively remote.

DOUBLE-CRESTED CORMORANT

This bird, one of six North American cormorant species, is related to the pelicans and boobies and like them is an ex-

Although the cormorant is a fine swimmer, diving underwater in search of fish, the bird does not have preen glands to help waterproof its wings and must "hang them out to dry" after each swim. (Phyllis Greenberg)

Naturalists are always pleased to see a young brown pelican, here attended by one of its parents, since the species has recently suffered a reduction in numbers because of pollution. (M. P. Kahl; see page 23.)

One of the most striking characteristics of the frigatebird is its bright-red throat pouch, which the male inflates during the breeding season to attract a mate. (George Holton)

cellent diver, fishing in large flocks along both coasts, although it is also found inland wherever fish are plentiful. Cormorants do not have sizable air sacs; in fact, they can even compress air *out* of their feathers to enable them to swim underwater. Unlike most other water birds, however, they do not have waterproof feathers and must hold their wings open in the sun to dry them after swimming. Cormorants are such skillful fishers that they have been used by man for many years, especially in the Far East, to capture fish. Bands are placed around their necks to prevent them from swallowing their catch.

MAGNIFICENT FRIGATEBIRD

Like their relatives the cormorants, frigatebirds have non-waterproof feathers, but because they cannot take off from water, they rarely touch the water at all, preferring to catch fish from the air, either spearing them in the water or stealing them from other seabirds, a habit that gave them their piratical name. They are wonderful fliers, with sail-like wings that enable them to fly through heavy storms. Unlike most other seabirds, frigatebirds do not migrate for great distances but remain relatively close to their nesting areas. The magnificent frigatebird is the only member of the family to breed in North America (in Key West, where a special refuge has been set aside for them), though they also can be found in Pacific islands, the Caribbean, and off South America. They are highly gregarious and nest in colonies. The male has developed a spectacular way of attracting mates. He sits on the nest making loud calls to the females flying above and inflates a red throat sac that resembles a large balloon. As soon as the eggs are ready for incubation, the sac deflates, although it is still visible against the bird's black plumage.

SKUA

More closely related to gulls than to frigatebirds, skuas (and their close relatives the jaegers) share the same habit of stealing food from other birds, chasing and attacking them

The herring gull is common along the shores of the Atlantic and Pacific and is often thought of as a pest, but in flight it is a beautiful sight indeed. (Pat Lynch)

until the fish is dropped or disgorged. They have hooked bills and sharp claws like hawks and other birds of prey and will also kill small seabirds and feed on carrion. They spend much of their time at sea and are good, strong fliers. The skua does not nest in North America, though it can be seen off the Atlantic coast; it is the only bird in the world that has populations nesting in both the Arctic and the Antarctic.

HERRING GULL

This species is perhaps the most widely distributed member of the gull family in North America and is a common sight on the Atlantic coast. A large gull, with a wingspan of nearly five feet, the herring gull is also known as the sea gull, though it does not spend nearly as much time at sea as its cousin the skua. It shares the skua's predatory habits in that it will feed on young birds, eggs, and dead animals, though it is not so aggressive in stealing food. Generally speaking, gulls eat almost anything, including shellfish,

which they drop on rocks to crack the shells, and they are fine scavengers, foraging in dumps and waterfront areas as well as following fishing boats for discarded food. Gulls appear to be unafraid of humans and are very gregarious, nesting in colonies and feeding in groups, making many different kinds of calls to communicate with each other. There are several species of gulls in North America, including the laughing gull of the east coast, the Heermann's gull of the west coast, and Franklin's gull, which is commonly found in the midwest on prairies during the summer.

ARCTIC TERN

Terns are smaller members of the gull family with long pointed wings and deeply forked tails. They do not soar as gulls do but fly with constantly flapping wings and are very graceful in the air. Their bills are not hooked, as gulls' are, and they are more selective feeders, diving to catch small fish from heights of thirty to forty feet. Terns are exceptionally noisy, and they too live in groups, often nesting di-

rectly on the sand with no special nest. They actively defend their nesting sites against predators, sometimes "dive-bombing" intruders who get too close. The arctic tern nests throughout the northern parts of the world but unlike other terns makes an exceptionally long migration, wintering in areas of the southern hemisphere and traveling more than ten thousand miles twice a year between summer and winter quarters in search of the cold-water crustaceans that are its favored food.

COMMON PUFFIN

Members of the auk family are the northern hemisphere's answer to the penguin, equipped with thick, waterproof feathers enabling them to dive and swim for their food. Unlike penguins, all auks (except for the extinct great auk) can fly, except at molting time, when they lose all of their flight feathers at once. The puffin, like its cousins the murres and auks, is a relatively squat bird with webbed feet, but unlike them has a very distinctive, parrotlike bill that becomes brightly colored during the breeding season. This bill is constructed in such a way that the bird can carry as many as thirty small fishes at one time when feeding its young. Puffins nest in colonies and lay their eggs in burrows for safety; both males and females feed the single chick, which can eat its own weight in fish a day, and then they abandon it after about six weeks. The chick fasts in the burrow for another week and then swims out to sea, eventually flying and diving for fish on its own.

This pair of arctic terns is performing a courtship display. Twice a year this bird migrates more than ten thousand miles between summer and winter quarters. (Townsend P. Dickinson)

The common puffin of the North Atlantic is a very uncommon sight because its breeding grounds are remote in the far north. It is the arctic counterpart of the penguin. (Kenneth W. Fink)

BIRDS OF THE SHORE

The American oystercatcher can be seen
on beaches in North America and in South
America as well, for its migration is a long
one, like that of many shorebirds.
(M. P. Kahl)

Many birds can be seen along the shores of North America; some of them we have met as seabirds and some of them we will meet in later chapters as marsh or water birds. All of the birds in this chapter, however, spend most of their time on the shore itself, wading in shallow seawater or on the mud flats and sandy beaches that provide so much food at low tide. Most of these birds are migratory, nesting in the far north and flying as far as the southern tip of South America in winter. Unlike the seabirds, most have long legs and are quite shy of humans, although they can easily be seen from a distance on beaches as they travel from their nesting sites to their wintering grounds.

The American avocet uses its distinctive upcurved bill to dig up insects as it wades through the water. Although it is a common sight along the coast, the bird can also be found inland; this one is wading on the shore of Great Salt Lake in Utah. (G. C. Kelley; see page 34.)

AMERICAN OYSTERCATCHER

This handsome bird was once a relatively common sight along the Atlantic coast north to Canada and southwest to Baja California, but is now seen only infrequently, although nesting activities have been reported since the 1960s in Massachusetts and on Long Island. One of two species of the oystercatcher family native to North America, the bird is well named, since its long red bill is constructed with a sharp tip that it uses to pry shellfish from rocks and to break the strong muscles that keep the shells closed. In addition to oysters and clams, the oystercatcher also eats sea urchins, crabs, and other marine animals found along the shore. These birds gather in groups, wading, swimming, and running quickly along the shore looking for food. They are good fliers but do not migrate long distances, usually remaining in the same range where they

The killdeer (left) and the black-bellied plover (right) are members of the same shorebird family and yet they live very different lives. The killdeer often lives far from the water in meadows, while the plover nests in the arctic tundra and spends much of its time traveling along the coast to its wintering grounds.
(H. F. Flanders, left;
Anthony Mercieca, right)

breed. Like many gregarious birds, they are noisy, making several different types of calls to communicate with their own kind.

BLACK-BELLIED PLOVER

Although the plover family is classified as one of the shorebird groups, few of its members actually spend much of the time on or near salt water. The killdeer, the most widely distributed plover, is completely at home far from the sea in meadows and upland pastures, while the mountain plover is primarily found in the plains and semidesert areas of the west. The black-bellied plover, however, is a true shorebird, feeding on insects and small shellfish in mud flats and salt marshes as well as around inland fields and lakes. These hardy birds, with short bills and compact

The spotted sandpiper is one of a large number of similar birds that are commonly found on the seashores of North America. (O. S. Pettingill, Jr.)

snipes, willets, curlews (the largest sandpipers), and woodcocks. They are more slender than the plovers, with longer bills and legs. Some members of this family make long migratory flights, usually in large flocks, and they are commonly seen along the coasts of both Pacific and Atlantic oceans on their way north or south. They can fly rapidly (some species have been clocked at more than a hundred miles per hour) but feed along the edge of the water for insects, small crustaceans, and tiny fish. The spotted sandpiper is one of the most common shorebirds in America and lives on fresh water as well as along the seashore. It resembles many of the other sandpipers, which are notoriously difficult to identify. The bird has many charming descriptive nicknames—gutter snipe, sand snipe, peep, seesaw, teeter peep, and tilt-up—and is one of the few species of birds in which the female is not only more aggressive than the male but is known to have more than one mate and leaves most of the incubation and chick-raising responsibilities to the male. The chicks are precocial, fully feathered, and ready to find their own food soon after hatching, but the parents usually keep them in tow for the first few weeks, teaching them where to feed.

bodies like the other plovers, nest in the arctic tundra in nests made of moss and lichen and migrate south for the winter via the Pacific and Atlantic shorelines, as well as through the Mississippi Valley. They travel in flocks and have distinctive voices (the killdeer is especially vocal and is named after one of its calls). Like many other ground-nesting birds, the plovers have developed a means of protecting their young by pretending to be crippled as they flop away from the nest and thus attracting the attention of predators to themselves.

SPOTTED SANDPIPER

The sandpiper family is very large, with more than fifty species native to North America, and includes not only the various species of sandpipers but also godwits, sanderlings,

The northern phalarope behaves more like a seabird than a shorebird, since it spends much time over the ocean, nesting in the far north and migrating as far as South America for the winter. (Roger Tory Peterson; see page 34.)

AMERICAN AVOCET

The avocet family includes both avocets and stilts, both distinguished by their very long legs and long slender bills. The American avocet, which is often seen inland around freshwater lakes and marshes as well as along the Pacific shore, is especially graceful, thanks to its upcurved bill and striking coloration. Although they can swim and will dive after food, they are most often found wading, often in cooperative groups, moving their upcurved bills from side to side as they stir up insects and crustaceans from the bottom.

NORTHERN PHALAROPE

Like the avocets, phalaropes are shorebirds that are often found inland far from shore, although the northern phalarope is truly oceanic, unlike most of its relatives. It is a small bird with a long bill and slender legs, a good flier, and a fine swimmer that spends much of its time over the ocean. This species has salt glands like the seabirds and a dense layer of feathers for insulation, since it migrates widely from the northern tundra all over the world, spending its winters at sea. The phalarope feeds on insects, plankton, and tiny crustaceans, running like a sandpiper on shore and feeding like a duck on the water, pecking at the water or tipping up to feed beneath the surface. Phalaropes practice role reversal: The females are larger and more brightly colored and initiate courtship, after which they leave the males to incubate the eggs and raise the young.

BLACK SKIMMER

Members of the skimmer family include three coastal species, one of which is native to North America. The name comes from the bird's habit of skimming along the surface

The black skimmer has an unusual method of feeding; it flies along with the lower half of its bill in the water, and when it strikes a fish, the upper bill snaps shut.
(Tom Bledsoe)

of the water with the lower half of the bill submerged. When the lower bill, immovable unlike that of other birds, strikes a fish or a crustacean, the head snaps down so that the upper part of the bill grasps the prey; the bird then drags it from the water and swallows it while still in flight. Black skimmers nest along the Atlantic coast, in the Gulf of Mexico, and on the Pacific coast from Mexico south. They rarely swim or dive but are graceful fliers; they move in flocks and rest during the daytime along beaches or sandbars.

OSPREY

The osprey is a bird of prey that feeds mainly on fishes and is classified in a family of its own in the Falconiformes order, which also includes hawks and falcons. Its feet are constructed somewhat differently from those of these other raptors, with a special, spiky covering on the pads of the toes to grip slippery fish, and its feathers are thick and compact to reduce waterlogging when it dives after prey. The osprey flies well above the water, hovering when it sights a fish and then diving at great speed. Because so much marine life has been affected by the presence of insecticides and other pollutants in the environment, ospreys have suffered a decline in population, much like the brown pelican, although their numbers now seem to be increasing. Osprey nests are common sights along the coast—heavy constructions of sticks, bones, seaweed, and other materials built on rocks, trees, and manmade structures to which osprey pairs will return for years to raise their young. The bald eagle, a true member of the hawk family, also feeds primarily on fish, usually in freshwater lakes and rivers, and it will often steal food from the smaller osprey where their ranges overlap.

The osprey, like its hawk relatives, is a powerful flier. This bird is bringing a fish back to the nest to feed its mate, which is incubating the eggs. (Tom & Pat Leeson)

BIRDS OF THE MARSH

The arrival of the red-winged blackbird in the north in February or March is a sure sign that spring is not far behind. (Gregory K. Scott; see page 44.)

Many dedicated bird-watchers find that high rubber boots are as important a part of their gear as a pair of binoculars, for the favorite habitat of many bird species is the wetland around lakes, rivers, and the shorelines of North America. As freshwater bodies of water fill with decaying vegetation, they become shallower, so that grasses and other plants may gain a foothold. These swamps are rich in insects, fish, and other marine life, attracting many birds, who find abundant food there. As the swamps become richer in organic matter, trees and shrubs become the dominant plants—forming a marsh—and this, too, is an environment that many species of birds find attractive. Some of these birds are only visitors, stopping briefly on their migratory flight or traveling there in search of food when it is scarce elsewhere, but a

large number of birds seem to spend most or all of their time in these wet places and we shall meet them in this chapter, so keep your boots handy.

SNOWY EGRET

This lovely member of the heron family is named for the long white plumes, called aigrettes, that it grows during the breeding season; these feathers were once so prized by milliners for ladies' hats that the birds were nearly extinct by the early twentieth century. They have made a comeback, however, under protection of the law and are seen now over a wider range—from the southern states north to Canada along the shore and in marshlands near the coast. Egrets are smaller than herons but have a similar appearance, with very long legs and a long curved neck. They wade in shallow water, darting after fish that they stir up

The great blue heron is a large, magnificent bird. It spends much of the day in this characteristic sunning position. (Stephen Collins; see page 38.)

The snowy egret, a small member of the heron family, has beautiful breeding plumes, which were once sought after by humans for decoration. The hunting severely reduced the bird's numbers in nature. (Tom Bledsoe)

from the bottom with their feet. Sometimes snowy egrets will fish from the air, dropping down quickly to catch their prey. Like other egrets, they also feed on insects and can sometimes be found inland with their close relatives the cattle egrets, waiting for the flies and grasshoppers kicked up by horses and cows in pasturelands.

GREAT BLUE HERON

This large heron (four feet tall) is one of the most widespread and best-known members of the heron family. It nests from Alaska and Canada to the Caribbean and winters over much of the same area, a common sight in marshes and alongside lakes, streams, and the seashore, standing in shallow water waiting for fish to come within reach. It is interesting to note that herons in northern waters where fish are less abundant will eat almost anything they can catch, whereas in the south, they can afford to be

more particular and will go after fish of only a certain size or species. Heron nests are large stick platforms lined with grasses, leaves, and pine needles. Built on the ground, in treetops, on ledges, and in shrubs, they are often used for years. The female heron will lay three or four eggs, which she and her mate incubate for about twenty-eight days. The parents feed their young by regurgitating fish into their mouths. Herons were once accused by fishermen of preying on game fish, but it has been found that they compete very little for the species that fishermen prize and will also eat amphibians, insects, small birds, and mammals.

WOOD STORK

Storks are relatives of herons and like them are tall and have long legs, but they have thick bills and bare faces and fly with their necks fully extended rather than curved. Storks prefer to nest in trees, although the white stork of

The wood stork lives in the swamps of Florida and other southern states, wading in the water in search of food. It builds its nest high in cypress trees. (Bill Dyer)

The whooping crane is one of the world's rarest birds, as well as America's tallest.
There are now major conservation efforts to save the species from extinction,
a possibility caused primarily by destruction of its habitat.
(Sam C. Pierson, Sr.; see page 43.)

The roseate spoonbill, a member of the ibis family, is named for the unique shape of its sensitive bill, which is perfectly designed to feel for fish underwater.
(Stephen J. Krasemann)

Europe nests almost entirely on rooftops. There is one native American stork, the wood stork, once called the wood ibis, and it is found only in Florida, where it nests in swamps. Wood storks are very wary and difficult to find, not only because they are shy but also because they are becoming increasingly rare, as the cypress trees in which they nest are cut down for lumber and as the water table in Florida is drained and lowered. Storks will feed alongside egrets and herons, wading in freshwater ponds and marshes and groping in the mud for fish, frogs, insects, and even baby alligators. Storks nest in colonies, and both parents are responsible for feeding their three or four offspring; it is estimated that a pair of storks will carry about fifty pounds of fish to each baby stork before it leaves the nest. There is no evidence that storks also carry human babies, though this myth relating to Europe's white stork is a very popular part of our culture.

ROSEATE SPOONBILL

This unusual-looking bird is the largest member of the ibis family, distinguished by its beautiful plumage and its spoon-shaped bill that is perfectly designed for feeding. As the spoonbill wades through the water, the bill moves from side to side underwater and snaps shut the moment its delicate nerve ends touch living prey. Spoonbills, like the ibises and their close relatives the storks and herons, feed on fish, crustaceans, and other aquatic life in tidal ponds and freshwater marshes in the Everglades and along the Gulf Coast states. Like other birds in this habitat, they have been severely affected by pollution and habitat destruction, but they are strictly protected and their numbers seem to be increasing. The relationship between the ibis and humans is a particularly old one; in ancient Egypt the sacred ibis, now extinct, was worshiped and even mummified in temples. Unlike the spoonbill, other ibises have slender bills with pointed tips. They are gregarious and often fly in V-shaped formations with their necks extended, like storks. The roseate spoonbill, like its cousin the scarlet ibis and the more distantly related flamingo, has conspicuous colors that seem to have nothing to do with camouflage or breeding display; perhaps these feather colors make it easier for the birds to flock together.

WHOOPING CRANE

Like the ibises, cranes are a very old group of birds—dating back perhaps 60 million years to the Eocene period—and yet they may not be able to survive to the twenty-first century because of hunting and habitat destruction, as humans drain the cranes' habitats of marshlands and wet prairies in order to build up farmlands and cities. There are two species of crane native to North America: the sandhill crane and the whooping crane, one of the rarest birds in the world. Although whooping cranes were never numerous and were always relatively restricted in their nesting and wintering grounds, increased human civilization reduced their numbers to a mere fifteen birds in 1937. Now, thanks to a concerted effort by biologists and the federal government, there are nearly a hundred birds in existence, a number of them raised in captivity by sandhill crane foster parents. The whooping crane is perhaps our tallest bird, at five feet in height, and is pure white with black wing tips and facial markings. They are stately birds, flying in spectacular V-formations and feeding in small groups on fish, crustaceans, small amphibians, and some vegetation. Whooping cranes perform wonderful courtship dances before nesting and are thought to mate for life. Although they are relatively long-lived (one captive lived over twenty-four years), they do not breed until at least three years of age and produce at the most two chicks a year, so we cannot expect their population to increase quickly, even with human help.

VIRGINIA RAIL

The rail family is related to the cranes and includes thirteen species in North America, such as the American coot (as aquatic a bird as most ducks), the gallinules (often called marsh hens, since they vaguely resemble chickens), and the rails. Rails are small birds with slender bodies that enable them to slip through narrow gaps in the dense vegetation of the freshwater marshes where they live; they are not strong fliers but may migrate long distances. The Virginia rail nests throughout southern Canada and the United States and is relatively common but rarely seen because it is shy and solitary, unlike most of the birds we have met in this book so far. Its call is distinctive, however, especially in the

The Virginia rail is not restricted to that state but nests as far north as Canada and winters as far south as Central America. (Rod Planck)

evening and at night, so the bird is quite often heard. The rail can swim well but prefers to run when pursued. The Virginia rail has a long bill that it uses to probe the mud for insects and other aquatic life, as well as some seeds.

RED-WINGED BLACKBIRD

Unlike the rail, this species is one of the most visible birds and is thought by some scientists to be the most numerous land bird on the continent. The males migrate from the southern states to the north in February or March and are one of the earliest arrivals, establishing a territory in a freshwater marsh to await the females. They are very aggressive and vocal in defending their territories, often at-

tacking much larger birds. In the late summer red-winged blackbirds join with other species, including starlings and grackles, to create enormous "blackbird" flocks that roost in the winter quarters in the south, often to the dismay of human residents, who are troubled by the noise and the droppings; one year, experts estimated that there were as many as 15 million birds at Dismal Swamp, Virginia. Nevertheless, these birds feed primarily on insects and weed seeds, so they do benefit humans in many ways. One of the redwing's winter companions is its close relative the cowbird, also a member of the troupial family, which also includes the Baltimore (or American) oriole and the meadowlarks. Troupials are in the passerine order, the most recently evolved group of birds and also the largest.

EVERGLADE KITE

There are a number of birds of prey that can be seen in marshy areas, including the osprey, the bald eagle, the marsh hawk, and the red-shouldered hawk, all of which are species whose numbers have been seriously reduced in recent years because of pesticides and the loss of habitat. The most endangered of the marsh species, however, is the everglade kite, which nests in the freshwater marshes of southern Florida and was reduced to as few as twenty birds in 1964. One of the reasons for this bird's rarity is that it is one of the most specialized feeders in the world, living exclusivly on a certain type of snail, and so it is restricted in range to areas where that snail exists. The kite is a relatively small hawk, with a wingspan of only forty-five inches (the osprey's wingspan may be six feet), and it is blue-black in color. Like all hawks, the kite has excellent eyesight and searches for its prey from the air, often perching or flying at heights of thirty feet or more. Once the kite catches a snail in its talons, it will hold the shell in one foot and extract the meat with its bill. Thanks to the efforts of conservationists, the bird is now completely protected by law and its numbers, while still small, are steadily increasing.

The everglade kite, a member of the hawk family, is a very specialized feeder, living exclusively on a type of snail that can be found in the swamps of southern Florida.
(M. P. Kahl)

BIRDS OF LAKE AND STREAM

The dipper is classified as a songbird and yet is adapted to life on the water, preferring mountain streams and ponds. Since it is not a good surface swimmer, it usually wades into the water before it dives in for fish and other food. (Jeff Apoian; see page 53.)

All of the birds we have met in this book so far have been water birds, living almost exclusively on or near salt or fresh water. Although the water birds in this chapter are occasionally seen along the coast or in freshwater swamps, especially on their migratory routes north and south, they are far more commonly found on the lakes and rivers of North America, swimming and diving for their food. Many of them migrate long distances from the northern regions where they breed to the southern United States and Mexico, and they can be seen regularly on their journeys as they follow certain flyways twice a year. The waterfowl, or members of the duck family, are among the most studied of all birds, partly because they are the most frequently hunted

and domesticated and partly because they make up such a fascinating and varied group, including swans and geese as well as many different types of ducks.

COMMON LOON

Although loons spend much of their time on freshwater lakes diving for fish as well as other aquatic life, sometimes making dives as deep as two hundred feet, they are not ducks but members of the oldest-known group of birds, dating back 65 million years to the Paleocene era. The loon is not only a powerful flier but it also is an especially strong swimmer, with webbed feet, a streamlined body, and mostly solid rather than hollow bones that help it submerge in the water. As they swim, loons use both feet at once to paddle rather than using one after the other, as ducks do, and they can move very quickly underwater, like the auks,

The common loon is one of the oldest species of birds, an inhabitant of lakes in the north during the summertime and of southern coastal areas during the winter. (Charlie Ott)

using their wings for steering. Almost incapable of walking on land, the loon must take off into the air by running along the water for twenty yards or more.

The common loon nests in the northern United States and Canada, as well as in Greenland and Iceland, building its nest as close to the water as possible. It migrates alone or in small groups as far south as the Gulf Coast. In winter, loons frequent saltwater beaches and coastal waters, but most of the year they prefer remote lakes far from human habitation, where their haunting laughlike calls may be heard for miles across the water in the evening or early morning.

HORNED GREBE

The grebe family is one of the most ideally adapted for life on the water. Although grebes resemble loons and ducks, and share many of their characteristics, they are not related to either family. Grebes are weak fliers but very strong div-

ers and swimmers, spending most of their life on the water even as chicks. They cannot dive until they are a few weeks old but are carried shortly after hatching by the parents as they search for food. They do not have wide bills like ducks but short, straight bills for snapping up insects and small fish, which they chase underwater. The horned grebe is capable of exceptionally deep dives and can stay underwater for up to three minutes. This species nests alone or in small colonies, building nests right on the water attached to grasses or reeds. Although it is a poor flier, the horned grebe will migrate from its nesting areas in Alaska and Canada south to the coasts of the United States.

ANHINGA

This single North American member of the anhinga family, also called the snakebird because of its small snakelike head on a long snaky neck, could be considered a freshwater version of the cormorant, since it shares the same habit of spreading its wings to dry after fishing underwater, having no natural waterproofing like other water birds. Anhingas have a long sharp bill for spearing their prey, which includes freshwater crustaceans, amphibians, and snakes. They live near sheltered lakes, slow-moving rivers, and marshes in the southern United States, often joining herons and egrets at nesting time, and they are often seen perching on branches to watch for fish. When they spot prey, they will dive from the perch or from the air. They are graceful fliers and excellent swimmers, equipped like grebes with the ability to control the air in their bodies, enabling them to float high on the water or to sink beneath and swim with only their heads and necks visible.

TRUMPETER SWAN

Although swans are quite different in appearance from mallard ducks, for instance, they are members of the same family and actually resemble ducks in many ways, with webbed feet, a rounded flat bill, dense plumage, a long

The horned grebe, named for its earlike tufts, is one of the most aquatic of all freshwater birds and even makes its nest on the water, supported by reeds and bushes. (Harry Engels)

neck, and short legs. All members of the family are strong fliers, migrating in large flocks twice a year, and they are beautifully adapted to life on the water. The trumpeter swan is the largest member of the family in North America and perhaps the most graceful, creating a lovely picture as it sails elegantly along the surface of the water. Swans rarely dive, although the trumpeter is capable of swimming underwater, and in the air it is capable of speeds of eighty miles per hour in a good wind.

This was once a common species, ranging from nesting areas in Alaska and Canada to its winter range in the northern United States, but because of man's hunting for their feathers and meat, and for sport, the trumpeter was nearly wiped out in the nineteenth century. Once numbering only sixty-six birds (in the 1930s), the bird has—thanks to the efforts of conservationists—made a dramatic comeback and is now thought to number as many as five thousand.

The swan's name comes from its exceptional voice, which can be deafening at close range and carries for miles. Its cousin the mute swan, an imported species familiar to park visitors, is, true to its name, relatively quiet, though it is exceedingly aggressive and will hiss fiercely. The mute swan, distinguished by an orange upper bill from the native black-billed American swans, has become feral or wild in several parts of the United States, and this may be a cause for worry if it drives native swans and geese from their breeding areas. The other two North American swans are the whistling swan (which hoots rather than whistles) and the whooper swan (which really whoops or bugles), only rarely seen here as a visitor from Iceland.

SNOW GOOSE

Geese are smaller than swans, have shorter necks, and are usually darker in color, although the snow goose—which nests in the Arctic—is white. (There is also a blue phase of the same species, which seems to be increasing in frequency, perhaps because its survival rate is greater in areas

The anhinga, a relative of the grebe and cormorant families, is a fine swimmer. It spears fish on its sharp, pointed bill. (Robert Bornemann)

The trumpeter swan is the largest swan in the world and has a voice to match. It was once nearly extinct but has made a remarkable recovery, thanks to the efforts of conservationists. (John M. Burnley; see page 48.)

The snow goose, which is as white as the snow on the arctic tundra where it nests, is highly gregarious like most water birds and nests in large colonies. (Farrell Grehan)

south of the snow-covered polar region.) Like swans, geese can utter loud, trumpeting noises and are social birds, traveling in flocks and mating for life. Because their feet are placed farther forward under their bodies, geese are more agile on land than swans or ducks and will often graze far from the water, feeding on grass, grain, and other plants. The familiar Canada goose, with its distinctive cheek patches, is the largest North American goose and also the most numerous; the snow goose is smaller, with a wingspread of five feet or less.

Geese, unlike many other birds, form very strong bonds, the pairs remaining together throughout the year. Although the female incubates the eggs herself, the male will often stand guard and then accompany the family as they search for food together. One particularly interesting characteristic of many members of the duck family among other birds, studied by Nobel Prize winner Konrad Lorenz with the European graylag goose, is "imprinting," a means by which a bond is formed between the young goslings and the parents, usually only the female, during the first day of life. Once the youngster has imprinted on the mother, it will recognize and follow her, assuring its own safety and access to food. So strong is this instinct that young goslings can be imprinted on humans if the true parents are not present. The goslings usually remain with their parents until the nesting season the following year, at which point they join groups of other yearlings to travel until they return to their original nesting sites at two or three years of age, at which time they form their own families.

WOOD DUCK

The mallard is probably the most recognizable species of duck, but it is only one of many that are native to North America. There are five major groups of ducks. Whistling ducks are large and rather like geese, with long necks and an ability to get about on land as well as water. The stiff-tailed ducks, such as the ruddy duck, are grebelike and highly aquatic. The dabbling ducks, which are surface

The wood duck feeds in fresh water by tipping its head down to reach the aquatic vegetation on which it lives. The male is one of the most beautiful ducks in the world. (Pat & Tom Leeson)

feeders, are smaller and include the best-known species, such as the mallard, pintail, teal, and wood duck. The diving or sea ducks, including the bufflehead, canvasback, and scaup, spend more time in salt water than in fresh. Finally, the mergansers are diving, fish-eating ducks. Of these groups, the dabbling ducks are the most numerous in North America, and the male wood duck in breeding plumage is arguably the most beautiful duck of them all.

Like many other dabblers, the wood duck nests near forested lakes, streams, or swamps in southern Canada and the northern United States, wintering in the south after migrating in small flocks. They feed primarily on aquatic vegetation, acorns, and other nuts, as well as insects and small amphibians. Dabbling ducks feed by swimming about on the surface of shallow water, tipping their tails up to reach for food underwater. They tend to prefer bodies of water surrounded with trees and weeds, presumably because plant life is richer there and because they are capable—unlike the diving ducks—of taking off from the water into the air without needing a running start.

Because of habitat loss and hunting—for the wood duck is a favorite target of duck hunters—the species was nearly extinct early in the century. Legal protection of both the duck and the forests in which it lives has steadily increased the population to several million, although experts feel that the numbers may drop again as humans expand their use of wilderness areas.

BUFFLEHEAD

Because most of the diving ducks are adapted to salt water, with nasal salt glands and dense plumage, they are called sea ducks and tend to winter in coastal, saltwater areas, although they usually breed inland on open bodies of fresh water in the northern United States and Canada. The bufflehead is the smallest diving duck—weighing about a pound (a male canvasback may weigh nearly three pounds)—and is one of the best divers, swimming underwater to feed on insects and also small fish, crustaceans, and a few plants. Diving ducks have large feet and small legs set far back on the body, making them awkward on land; and their wings are smaller, requiring them to run on the water before they can take off, although they are strong fliers once in the air. (The bufflehead is the only diving duck that can take off immediately, perhaps because of its small size.)

The female bufflehead is gray-brown with a small white cheek patch, and she prefers to lay her eggs in tree holes

The bufflehead is a diving duck that seems to be at home in salt water as much as in fresh. The male and the female, like many other members of the duck family, do not resemble each other but have distinctive markings and coloration. (David O. Hill)

The belted kingfisher male and female look alike, although the female is more colorful; they appear to share the duties of incubating eggs and raising young equally.
(Stephen J. Krasemann)

made by flickers or other birds close to a lake or river. The male, which is larger and appears not to assist in raising the young, is mostly white with a black back and a large puffy "buffalo" head that gives the species its name.

KINGFISHER

Not all species in the kingfisher family are fishers; some live far from the water and feed primarily on insects. The belted kingfisher, however, the largest of the six North American species, is usually found near water, perched on a branch or hovering over the water watching for the small fish or amphibians on which it feeds. The bird nests along creeks or streams in a burrow, often several feet deep, that it digs with its bill. It can be found in many parts of Canada and the United States wherever there is fresh water.

Like other kingfishers, this bird is striking looking, with a large crested head and a relatively small body with little feet. This is one of the few species in which the female is more brightly colored than the male. Unlike many of the

other water birds, kingfishers are solitary except at breeding time. Like many birds of prey, the kingfisher disposes of indigestible bones, scales, and other matter in small regurgitated pellets, which can sometimes be found lining its nest.

DIPPER

This bird is the single representative of the dipper family in North America and is the only member of the passerine or songbird order that is truly adapted for life on the water, with a thick plumage, preen glands for waterproofing, and a flap over the nostrils to keep water out. Dippers do not have webbed feet and are not good surface swimmers, but they usually wade into the water or dive from a perch or the air and are exceptionally fast underwater, where they feed on insect larvae. Seen only in the West, the dipper prefers mountain streams and will even nest in the stream itself, on a rock or under a waterfall. Dippers do not migrate in the fall but may move downstream during the winter when the water freezes.

BIRDS OF THE FOREST

This red-eyed vireo is a member of the vireo family, which is thought to have originated in the tropics, although some species nest in North America. The red-eyed vireo nests as far north as Canada but spends the winter along the Amazon River in South America. (Dan Sudia; see page 62.)

Some of the aquatic birds we have seen—such as the wood duck and the wood stork—can be found in areas where trees are predominant features of the landscape, but the birds in this chapter are truly adapted to life in the forest, whether it be the coniferous forests in the north and west or the deciduous woodlands of the east. Generally speaking, the variations in behavior, feeding habits, and appearance are far greater in forest birds than in the species we have met so far.

YELLOW-BILLED CUCKOO

This member of the cuckoo family can be found in forests throughout North America, except in the extreme north,

attracted by the rich variety of insect life there (principally caterpillars, which it eats in great quantities) and by the protection that foliage provides, since the bird is shy. It does not live in the deep forest but in thickets and heavy underbrush, where it conceals itself in the leaves, though it can often be located by its distinctive call, similar to the "cuckoo" sound of the European cuckoo, from which the family gets its name. Like its close relative the black-billed cuckoo, this bird is sometimes called a rain crow, because its call is thought to precede rainstorms.

WHIP-POOR-WILL

Another distinctive forest sound that gives the bird its name is that of the whip-poor-will, which can be found in woodlands in the east and southwest and which can be heard at night, uttering repetitive calls from a favorite sing-

The great horned owl is most often found in the forest, but it inhabits mountains, marshes, and deserts as well, nesting on cliffs, in hollow trees, and even on the ground when nothing better is available. (Leonard Lee Rue III; see page 56.)

This beautiful pileated woodpecker is perfectly adapted to a life in the trees where it spends most of its time. In searching for its food, especially its favorite, carpenter ants, the woodpecker will chisel out chips to get to the heart of a living tree, although it can also find its food in dead trees and by peeling bark and digging holes in stumps and fallen logs. (Leonard Lee Rue III; see page 58.)

ing perch, often for long periods of time (the record number of calls in a sequence is over a thousand, but fifty to a hundred is more common). This bird is in the nightjar family, which includes the nighthawk (not a true hawk), and it resembles an owl in flight, though it feeds primarily on insects. Like other members of the family, it is very difficult to see, because of its mottled coloration, and it feeds mostly at night, catching insects by holding its mouth open as it flies about near the ground. The whip-poor-will spends much time on the ground, especially during the day, when it dozes in the leaves, protected by its camouflaging plumage. The female lays her eggs directly on the ground without making a nest of any kind.

GREAT HORNED OWL

Another nocturnal species, the great horned owl, is common throughout much of North America, residing in all sorts of forested land from the Arctic to the southern tip of South America. It is one of the largest and most powerful members of the owl family, roosting by day in the treetops and hunting at night for rodents, rabbits, and many different types of birds, which it eats back at the roost, regurgitating pellets of undigested bones and hair or feathers. Like other owls, the great horned owl is a silent flier; its soft feathers muffle the sound of its wings, enabling it to listen for its prey.

The tufts on the owl's head are not ears, although its hearing is extremely acute, as is its vision, like that of other birds of prey. All birds have some binocular vision (the ability to see the same object with both eyes at once, like humans) as well as monocular vision (the ability to see with each eye independently), and because they are unable to turn their eyes in the sockets they must move their heads to see in different directions. Owls are unusual, however, in that their eyes face front, giving them exceptionally good binocular vision, and they can rotate their heads about three-quarters of a full circle to look around them. It was once thought that an owl could move its head all the way around its body, but this is not true; it simply whips the head from one extreme position to the other so quickly that it seems to keep rotating in only one direction.

This whip-poor-will looks a bit like an owl, and it too is most active at night, when its distinctive call can be heard repeatedly for several hours at a stretch. (Bill Dyer)

This yellow-billed cuckoo is sitting on its own nest, incubating its own eggs, although this species has been known to lay eggs in the nests of other birds, leaving them to be hatched and raised by foster parents. (Bill Dyer; see page 55.)

The blue jay is an impressive-looking bird with a temper to match, being one of the more aggressive songbirds. It is a member of the crow family and shares many traits with its intelligent, noisy cousins. (Ken Brate)

This hardy little bird, the black-capped chickadee, can live year-round in the northern forests, where it may be heard chattering and whistling its own name throughout the winter. (Russ Kinne)

PILEATED WOODPECKER

Members of the woodpecker family are unusual in that they have adapted to a life in trees much more successfully than any other group of birds. Although they fly well, they do not generally migrate or travel for long distances and seem to spend most of their existence clinging to the sides of trees with their short feet and sharp claws, propping themselves up with their strong tail. They feed primarily on insects that live within the bark, using their acute hearing to detect the insects and pecking at the tree with their hard, pointed bill. Woodpeckers have a very long sticky tongue, which they use to capture insects or lick sap (sapsuckers are members of the woodpecker family). They also use the bill to make holes for nesting and roosting and to drum or tap to attract mates or defend their territories, as a supplementary tactic to their harsh calls and cries.

There are many species of woodpeckers, including some that prefer one type of forest over another (the gila woodpecker of the southwest, for example), but most, including the pileated woodpecker, have adapted to many different types of wooded areas and are found throughout the continent, except in treeless areas of the far north and the mountains. Nevertheless, because of lumbering activities by humans, some species of woodpeckers have declined in numbers. One species, the ivory-billed woodpecker, is extremely rare, if not actually extinct.

BLUE JAY

This handsome crested bird doesn't look much like a crow, but it is a member of the crow family and shares many traits with the common crow, including high intelligence, an extremely noisy and aggressive manner, and a relatively bad reputation. Its most common call is a "jay" sound, but it has many different cries and the ability to mimic other species, including hawks, chickadees, orioles, and goldfinches. Blue jays, like crows, feed on many different kinds of food—acorns, nuts, seeds, fruits, and berries, as well as insects, small fish, and amphibians, and even small birds and their eggs. Because of this omnivorousness as well as their intelligence, they have been able to survive the loss of forested land by adapting to human-made environments, such as city parks and backyards.

Although known as robber jays for their nest-robbing behavior, blue jays feed only rarely on the eggs of other birds and in fact can do other species a great service by raising an alarm call when they see a predatory owl, which they will even attack in flight, or "mob," together with crows and other birds.

BLACK-CAPPED CHICKADEE

This is another commonly seen species in residential areas, tame enough to feed regularly at bird feeders but preferring the forests of the northern parts of the United States and of Canada. Although some chickadees migrate south, most are residents in their range, foraging for insects, as well as seeds and berries, in twigs and branches, where they can be seen fluttering about. They chatter and sing throughout the year and are named for their call note, "chicka-dee-dee-dee." This species is a member of the titmouse family, most of which nest in holes in trees, but is hardier than most, for it can withstand even severe winters.

RED-BREASTED NUTHATCH

The nuthatch family is closely related to the titmice and many species are also regular visitors to bird feeders and will nest in man-made birdhouses. They are small birds that cling to tree bark much as woodpeckers do, with sharp claws and short strong legs. Most nuthatches feed on insects, but the red-breasted nuthatch, which prefers the coniferous forests of the west and, in recent years, of the northeast, prefers seeds, which it extracts from pine cones with its thin, sharp bill. A close relative, the brown-headed nuthatch, is the first reported American bird to use a tool in feeding—a piece of bark that it holds in the bill to flake off other pieces of bark in search of insects. Nuthatches rarely migrate, but when food is scarce in winter the red-breasted nuthatch has been known to move in large flocks as far south as the Gulf of Mexico.

BROWN CREEPER

Like the nuthatches and woodpeckers, the brown creeper is well designed to cling to tree trunks in search of insects, using its tail as a prop. To get down, the creeper will flutter

The red-breasted nuthatch, like the chickadee, is also a winter resident in many areas and is a common sight at bird feeders. (Gunther A. Wachter)

The brown creeper is well adapted to tree life, like the woodpeckers, and can be found "creeping" along the underside of branches in search of many different kinds of insects that can be found there. (Dan Sudia)

down rather than climb, like the nuthatch, although it will hop backward and can "creep" along the underside of branches looking for food. The only member of the creeper family in North America, the brown creeper lives in both coniferous and hardwood forests across the United States and southern Canada and also ranges in Europe and Asia, where it lives in the same range as a very similar bird, the European brown creeper, which was once thought to be the same species, although the two birds seem to recognize the difference and rarely if ever interbreed.

CEDAR WAXWING

This distinctive-looking bird is remarkable in many ways. Like other waxwings, it forms a red waxlike substance on its wing tips, the function of which is unknown, and it is quite specialized in its diet, preferring fruits and berries, which causes it to be nomadic rather than truly migratory as it moves from place to place in search of its seasonally available food (though it will occasionally supplement its diet

with insects). Cedar waxwings can live in various kinds of forests and wooded land, usually traveling in small flocks and appearing in different areas unpredictably rather than on regular schedules. Cedar waxwings have an appealing ritual in courtship: They pass fruit or other food back and forth before one of them swallows it. When food is especially abundant, they will eat so much they can hardly fly, and they have been known to become intoxicated on over-ripe fruit.

NORTHERN SHRIKE

Like most of the birds in this chapter, the shrike family is part of the passerine or songbird order, but unlike the others, shrikes are predatory, feeding on small mammals, birds, and reptiles as well as insects. Known also as the butcher bird for its habit of impaling killed prey on thorns or twigs, the northern shrike is seen throughout the northern part of North America and in Europe and Asia as well, usually in coniferous forests, where it perches on the tops of trees

This handsome fruit-eating bird, the cedar waxwing, often nests in small colonies. Parental chores are relatively light (incubation is only about two weeks, and the young birds spend less than three weeks in the nest), except that most cedar waxwings have more than one family a year. (John S. Dunning)

watching for prey. Similar in habits to hawks and owls, and fierce in temperament, the shrike is preyed upon by those birds and is generally wary except when it is in pursuit of other birds, often those as large as itself.

RED-EYED VIREO

This species is unlikely to be a victim of the northern shrike, since it prefers the deciduous forests of southern Canada and the United States. Although its numbers have decreased somewhat in recent years, this bird was once one of the most abundant birds of the American forest, foraging in trees for insects, mostly caterpillars and moths, and nesting in tree forks sometimes as high as sixty feet above the ground. The species has the odd distinction of being one of the most common hosts for the brown-headed cowbird, which often lays its eggs in vireo nests and leaves them for the vireo to incubate and raise. It is also one of the most persistent singers, often singing throughout the summer months and even while eating. In 1954, one red-eyed vireo

was reported to sing 22,197 songs during a ten-hour period—surely some kind of a record!

AMERICAN REDSTART

The American wood warbler family, to which the redstart belongs, is one of the largest groups of songbirds in North America. Most species prefer woodlands or swampy areas for nesting. They are migratory, often traveling in great waves as they move north and south. All of the warblers are active, flitting about in search of insects, but the American redstart is especially animated, leaping into the air to catch flying insects, although it will also pick insects off leaves and occasionally dines on berries and seeds. Like the red-eyed vireo, the redstart is commonly a foster parent to the cowbird, since its nesting habits are similar. The male is more brightly colored than the female, which is gray and yellow rather than black and white with orange patches, but not so striking as the male of the painted redstart, a species of the southwest, which has bright-red patches but is otherwise very similar in its feeding habits, drooping its wings and fanning its tail as it climbs trees searching for food.

EVENING GROSBEAK

The finch family has more species in North America than any other, including cardinals, grosbeaks, juncos, sparrows, buntings, and towhees, and many of them are the best singers of all birds. As its name would imply, the evening grosbeak has a very large powerful bill, which it uses to crack tough seeds. Like the waxwings, evening grosbeaks tend to follow their food from season to season; capable of remaining north when seeds are available, the bird often moves in large flocks to different areas unpredictably, depending on the seed crop. Once rare in the eastern part of the continent, evening grosbeaks are now relatively common, thanks to the bird-feeding habits of humans and to the cultivation of seed-producing plants.

The evening grosbeak prefers to nest in the coniferous forests of Canada and the northern United States, building its nest of twigs in a cup shape in evergreen tree branches. Like many finches, the male grosbeak is more brightly colored than the female, but in this species both sexes sing courtship songs rather than just the male.

The evening grosbeak, which was once thought to sing in the evening, feeds on insects, but its favorite food includes the buds and seeds of many different kinds of deciduous trees. (Calvin Larsen)

BIRDS OF THE MEADOW

Sprague's pipit, a sparrow-sized bird, is not easy to see, since it spends much of its time hiding in the grass, but in summer the male performs remarkable feats of flying to attract a mate and to defend his territory. (Philip Boyer; see page 73.)

In this chapter we will meet a wider variety of birds than in any other, partly because the term "meadow" is used here in its broadest sense, encompassing once-forested lands now open because of lumbering and agriculture, as well as the vast grasslands or prairies in the midwest, which once supported few trees but now have occasional woodlands, thanks to human cultivation. Some of the birds seen in the meadows, therefore, are actually tree birds that have adapted to open areas, while others are species that have always lived on the ground or in sparsely forested land.

RED-TAILED HAWK

This hawk is one of the most commonly sighted, because it

The red-tailed hawk can spend hours soaring in the sky or perched on a tree or fence looking for its prey, but once a mouse or other small animal has been spotted, the hawk can swoop down and catch it in seconds. (Jeanne White)

is so widely distributed over North America, having adapted to nearly every possible habitat, except for the northern tundra and deep forest. It is also one of the largest hawks, with a wingspread of up to six feet. A spectacular flier, like all hawks, the red-tail soars high in the sky and hovers on thermals, or columns of warm air that rise upward from the ground (which is why red-tails are rarely seen in the cool morning air). It will also search for prey while seated on a perch near fields, taking off and gliding down to grasp the animal in its talons. It can fly up to 40 miles per hour and may accelerate to 120 miles per hour in dives.

The red-tailed hawk has exceptional eyesight, able to spot a mouse from a distance of half a mile. And, in fact, mice and other rodents are its principal diet. Nevertheless, the hawk has long been shot by humans, who fear damage to their poultry. Red-tailed hawks are territorial and monogamous and are thought to keep the same territories and

The ring-necked pheasant is a common sight in fields throughout many parts of North America, but it is a native of Asia, owing its existence here to its value as a game bird for hunters. (Neal Mishler)

mates for life. In courtship the hawk pair is very noisy and makes dramatic battlelike flights, diving and swooping in the air.

RING-NECKED PHEASANT

Another common sight in the open farmlands throughout the United States (except for the desert and the southeastern states) is this striking bird, a member of the pheasant family, which also includes the peacock, the partridge, the quail, and the jungle fowl, which is the ancestor of our domestic chicken. Unlike the hawk, however, the pheasant remains almost entirely on the ground, although it is capable of short flights, and rarely travels far from its nest feeding mostly on plants, seeds, nuts, and some insects. Like the hawk, this pheasant is a favorite target of hunters, but primarily for sport and food; rather than declining, the

The wild turkey, from which our Thanksgiving bird descended, was once so numerous that Benjamin Franklin believed it should be made our national bird. (Leonard Lee Rue III)

pheasant's population in North America is actually growing; in fact, the bird owes its very existence in North America to its status as a game bird, for it is not a native at all but was introduced here in the nineteenth century, first in California, though it has now become widely established and is even the state bird of South Dakota. The male is a beautiful bird, with iridescent head and neck, a crest, and spurs on its legs. The female is mottled brown, giving her good camouflage, since the eggs are laid on the ground in open fields and pastures.

WILD TURKEY

A close relative of the pheasant and the ancestor of our domesticated turkey, the wild turkey is the only North American representative of the turkey family and is now relatively rare in the wild, though it once numbered in the millions

The mourning dove, a cousin of the common pigeon, is one of America's most popular game birds, as was the now-extinct passenger pigeon, which was exterminated by hunters during the late nineteenth century. (Ken Brate)

before the arrival of Europeans, who hunted it to extermination over much of its range. The turkey was once so common, in fact, that Benjamin Franklin wanted it to be named our national bird, instead of the bald eagle, and John James Audubon selected it for the first plate in his famous illustrated book *Birds of America*. There are different populations of wild turkey in separate areas of the continent, each with slightly different characteristics; they are considered geographic races or subspecies.

The turkey is our largest game bird, standing perhaps four feet high with a five-foot wingspread. The males are larger than the females and flock separately from them in winter, but in spring attract mates by performing strutting displays and gobbling, a noise that can be heard for some distance. Turkeys nest on the ground and feed there as well, usually on seeds and nuts, though they will also take insects and even small amphibians and reptiles. Because their food is usually hard and often difficult to digest, turkeys have well-developed gizzards to grind their food.

MOURNING DOVE

The mourning dove, named for its sad-sounding coo, a song made by the male at breeding time, is a member of the pigeon family and may, in fact, have much to mourn, being one of America's most hunted game birds and a close relative of the passenger pigeon, which was hunted to extinction in 1899. Although the mourning dove is widespread, the only bird to nest in all forty-eight of the contiguous United States, it was never as populous as the passenger pigeon, which once numbered in the billions, making up perhaps 40 percent of *all* birds in the United States. Passenger pigeons once traveled in enormous flocks of several million, darkening the skies as they flew and taking up miles of forest, searching for nuts and acorns. It is incredible that so many birds could have been wiped out in so short a time—from the 1870s to the turn of the century—except that their flocking habits made them an easy target for hunters, who would sell them for food, and the elimination of forests left them little natural habitat.

Mourning doves migrate in much smaller flocks and are still common, though some 30 million are killed each year. They feed on seeds, usually in farmland, and though they roost in trees are not so dependent on large forests for their livelihood. The common pigeon of our cities is actually a rock dove native to Europe and Asia but introduced here in the seventeenth century as a domesticated species, raised for its meat and its homing abilities. Many rock doves are still raised in captivity for show and food, but many others have become feral, or wild, feeding in farmlands and cities, on grain, seeds, grasses, and whatever scraps of food they can find.

MONK PARAKEET

This is another introduced species, brought here as a cage bird but allowed to escape into the wild, where it became established in several areas in the northeast and Florida. Because the monk parakeet lives on seeds and grain, it is considered a pest in most agricultural areas and there have even been bounties offered to help control populations. They are native to South America but can survive mild winters in the north. They build their nests in trees, sometimes in pairs and sometimes in large communal groups of as many as twenty pairs.

It is interesting that the monk parakeet should have established itself here, because there was once a native North American parrot, the Carolina parakeet, which is now extinct. This brightly colored bird once ranged through the midwest and south but was killed off for its beautiful feathers and its habit of annoying farmers by eating corn and pecking at apples for the seeds and was hunted due to its popularity as a cage bird. Although the monk parakeet is in no danger of extinction, it has been eliminated from many areas where it had gone wild and North America may again be without any members of this intelligent, colorful family.

The handsome monk parakeet is actually a native of South America but has become wild in several parts of the United States, having escaped from cages. (Tom McHugh)

The barn owl, with its distinctive heart-shaped face, actually seems to prefer living in barns rather than the woods. (Peter & Stephen Maslowski)

BARN OWL

The barn owl, on the other hand, is usually greeted warmly by farmers when it takes up residence nearby (often in the barn itself), for it is an efficient hunter of mice and other rodents, as well as rabbits, bats, and some birds. Like other owls, it locates its prey by hearing, and it hunts mostly at night; unlike most other owls, it prefers open country to the forest, roosting in old buildings, caves, and burrows. Barn owls also have some structural differences from the other owls, mostly in the feet and in the distinctive heart-shaped face, which gives the bird a very curious appearance and causes scientists to put it into a family of its own separate from other owl species.

BARN SWALLOW

Another barn nester, the barn swallow, is also much loved by North Americans, mostly because of its useful habit of catching insects in fields and marshes. The bird has a distinctive forked tail, unlike other members of the swallow family, but like them is a superb flier, spending much of its time in the air, more than most other birds. Barn swallows feed in flight, holding their mouths open to scoop up insects, and are famous for their migrations, since they are usually the earliest arrivals in the spring, traveling in huge flocks, which can often be seen perching on wires or rooftops rather than trees. They often nest communally, building their nests of mud, clay, and grass, lined with poultry feathers or horsehair, which they pick up around the barns where they like to live.

The barn swallow, which also likes to nest in barns and other manmade structures, is a fine flier and usually catches its food (insects) on the wing. (Russell C. Hansen)

HORNED LARK

The meadowlark is actually a member of the troupial fam-
·ily, along with the red-winged blackbird (discussed in the
chapter on marsh birds), but the horned lark is a true lark,
the only native species of lark in North America. This bird
nests as far north as the arctic coasts of Alaska and Canada
and as far south as Mexico in the west and Georgia in the
east. It is a ground bird, living mostly in treeless open land,
and feeds on seeds and insects while walking or running.
The female builds her cup-shaped nest of grass in a hollow
on the ground in a territory established by the male who
sings while perched on a clump of earth or while flying,
sometimes at heights of eight hundred or more feet, as he
circles and then drops to earth.

MOCKINGBIRD

Like the larks, mockingbirds are fine singers, but as the
name implies they are known for singing songs that are not
their own. The mockingbird family also includes catbirds
and thrashers but is best known for the mockingbird itself, a
symbol of the south, and a superb mimic of many different
bird species as well as piano music and barking dogs. Not a
migratory bird, the mockingbird ranges over much of the
south but also resides as far north as Oregon and New-
foundland, fiercely defending its nesting territory against all
intruders. They prefer relatively open land at the edge of
the forests, in farmlands, in the desert, and in residential
areas, where they feed primarily on insects, berries, and
fruits.

The horned lark often perches on posts to sing its beautiful song. (Patrick Grace)

The mockingbird is also known for its song, as well as for its ability to mimic the songs of many other species. (Thomas W. Martin)

SPRAGUE'S PIPIT

The pipit family is distributed nearly worldwide but is relatively rare in North America, where it is represented by species that nest in the tundra of the arctic region. Sprague's pipit, however, nests farther south into the northern United States and winters in the southern states. The species was named by Audubon for Isaac Sprague, an artist who accompanied him along the Missouri River in 1848. The bird nests on the ground and spends much of its time there, hidden in the grass of the open prairies that it inhabits, feeding on seeds and insects, but the male is famous for his spectacular flights during the breeding season, when he will spiral upward to five hundred feet or so, making a sound much like a tiny set of sleigh bells before he plummets to the ground to meet the female.

STARLING

There are no native members of the starling family in North America, and yet this bird is one of the most commonly seen, having quickly established itself after being deliberately introduced from Europe into New York City in 1890 by a man who is said to have wanted to populate America with every species of bird mentioned in Shakespeare's works. Like the common house or English sparrow, another introduced species, the starling has become very widespread and populous, often to the point of pestiness, since it often roosts in residential areas and travels in huge flocks of blackbirds along with robins and other species. Like its relative the myna bird, the starling has a metallic sheen to its plumage in summer and is a surprisingly good mimic, even imitating the human voice. It competes with many native birds for food, which includes insects and weed seeds, as well as berries and some grain, and for nesting places in hollow trees, although the starling prefers open land to deep forest and will in urban areas nest on buildings. It is perhaps appropriate that the first-known nest in North America was built in the eaves of the American Museum of Natural History!

The starling, although not native to North America,
is one of our most common birds.
Its plumage takes a metallic sheen in summer,
as seen in this photograph. (Stephen Dalton)

BIRDS OF PRAIRIE AND DESERT

The burrowing owl is also adapted to life without trees, nesting in a hole in the ground, where it raises offspring which can, when disturbed, make a sound remarkably like that of a rattlesnake.
(Stephen J. Krasemann; see page 78.)

Several of the birds that like open country can be found in the semiarid prairies of the midwest or the dry desert country of the southwest. Although these, like all habitats, require special adaptations to food and climate, there are a number of species that prefer them, even as humans and other animals tend to avoid them. Most of the desert lands are created by a lack of rainfall and poor soil that cannot absorb rain when it does occur. The only plants that can survive there are those capable of retaining water or of doing with very little, and they are not dense enough to support much animal life; in addition, desert birds must cope with dramatic changes in temperature from night to day and from season to season and with strong sweeping winds as well.

This female phainopepla feeds crushed berries and insects to her young for about three weeks, until they are able to fend for themselves. (Anthony Mercieca; see page 82.)

SAGE GROUSE

The grouse family, which also includes prairie chickens and ptarmigans, is hardy and has adapted to many extreme habitats—above the tree line on mountains and on the tundra, the prairies, and deserts. They live mostly on the ground but are capable of flying short distances. The sage grouse, like its cousins, does not migrate but lives permanently in areas where sagebrush—on which it relies for food and shelter—is plentiful, in the western and southwestern states. This species performs a remarkable courtship display just before breeding: The males flock together in the early morning in a particular area on the ground and strut around, inflating colorful air sacs on their breasts and displaying their handsome plumage as they make loud noises to impress the females, who gather to watch. The dominant male will then breed with several females, who go off to

This male sage grouse is demonstrating his prowess to a group of females by strutting, pointing his tail feathers, and inflating air sacs in his breast. This amazing courtship display occurs each year on the same strutting arena, which he shares with as many as fifty or more other male grouse. (Tom Bledsoe)

The male vermilion flycatcher is another brightly colored bird that prefers the arid regions of the southwest; the female is much less colorful, mostly brown and black with only a little pink on her underside. (Sydney Bahrt)

make their nests in the ground, lined with underbrush, lay their eggs, and incubate them with no male assistance.

ROADRUNNER

We met the yellow-billed cuckoo as a forest dweller; the roadrunner is a member of the same family but has many habits that are very much its own. Although it can fly, it prefers to remain on the ground, where it runs very quickly after the insects on which it feeds, though it can also eat small rodents, snakes (including rattlesnakes), and occasional fruits. The open floor of the dry plains and deserts where it lives is ideal for running, and the bird has been known to move as fast as twenty miles per hour. It builds a nest of sticks lined with whatever it can find—from leaves to snakeskin—and it is believed that the bird mates for life, remaining in its territory throughout the year.

BURROWING OWL

Although this bird is very much an owl, like the roadrunner it has some special kinds of behavior that help it survive in the open prairie land. Like other owls, it hunts at night and catches some of its prey in flight, but it spends much of its time on the ground and even nests in a burrow, usually one abandoned by a prairie dog or other ground rodent, though it can build its own if necessary. Its call is similar to the roadrunner's and it, too, feeds primarily on insects and rodents; it will also take snakes, lizards, toads, and even small birds. Because prairie dogs have largely disappeared from their original range in the prairies of the west and midwest, the burrowing owl is not as common as it once was, though it can be found in prairie dog colonies in the northwest and west and in parts of the midwest. There is even a Florida burrowing owl that lives on the prairies in the center of the state.

COSTA'S HUMMINGBIRD

The hummingbird family is unusual in many ways; it is one of the largest groups, with well over three hundred species of very tiny birds, and there are many variations within the group, since these birds are extremely adaptable and can be found in many North American habitats, with the exception of the great treeless prairies of the midwest and the ocean. Hummingbirds are very small and have a very high metabolism, since they expend a great deal of energy flying, so they must feed almost constantly, usually on nectar and insects. Nevertheless, they are extraordinary athletes, capable of flying up and down as well as forward, backward, and sideways. (The name of the family comes from the humming noise they make as their wings move as they beat up to sixty times a second.) The ruby-throated hummingbird migrates across the Gulf of Mexico on its twice-yearly migration, feeding heavily before each trip to be able to survive the six-hundred-mile flight.

Costa's hummingbird (named for a French collector of hummingbirds) has adapted to life in the deserts of the west and southwest, feeding on nectar and insects found in various desert plants. It builds its nest on desert trees—cactus, sage, and yucca—and is capable of withstanding the cool desert nights by becoming torpid at that time, so that it does not need to use up so much energy. Like most other hummingbirds, Costa's is brightly colored, especially the male, and he performs a spectacular courtship display in flight, making high-pitched noises to attract his mate, who usually perches nearby to watch.

VERMILION FLYCATCHER

This brilliantly colored member of the tyrant flycatcher family (which also includes the phoebes and pewees, named for their calls) prefers the desert and semiarid regions of the southwestern states. Only the male is red (the female is mostly brown), and like the hummingbird he performs a courtship flight for his perching mate. Most other species in this family, which like the hummingbirds are thought to have originated in South America and gradually

Most cuckoos live in wooded areas, but the roadrunner, a member of the same family, is specially adapted to life in the treeless regions of the American southwest. (Tom McHugh)

Costa's hummingbird, one of the smallest members of the hummingbird family, has a wingspread of only 4 inches, yet it is a strong flier, capable of holding itself virtually motionless in the air as it feeds on nectar. (Anthony Mercieca; see page 78.)

moved north, are not as brightly colored as the vermilion flycatcher, but all of them are very aggressive for their small size and all of them—true to their name—feed on insects, which they usually catch in flight. Unlike the other birds we have seen in this chapter, this bird is migratory, like the other flycatchers, moving south to Mexico in the winter.

CACTUS WREN

Most species in the wren family are native to Central and South America, but there are ten in North America. One of them, the cactus wren, lives in the southwestern deserts. Like most wrens, this one is brownish and spends much of its time on the ground, actively hopping about looking for insects under leaves and rocks. It will also feed on berries and the fruit of cactus, though it gets its name from the fact that the nest is invariably built in a cactus. The bulb-

shaped nest is a complicated affair made of plant fibers and fur or feathers with a long entryway near the top. Like many wrens, the cactus wren builds a new nest every year but keeps old ones in good repair to use for roosting.

PHAINOPEPLA

The silky flycatcher family is related to the waxwings; there is no close biological relationship to the tyrant flycatchers, although the two families resemble each other in appearance and behavior to some extent. Only one member of the family lives in North America, the phainopepla, which nests in the deserts of California and the southwest. It is a handsome bird, with a crested head and glossy dark plumage (the female is gray). In spite of its flycatcher family name, the phainopepla actually prefers to feed on berries, especially mistletoe, although it does eat insects, which it

The black-throated sparrow, also called the desert sparrow, is one of several members of the finch family that lives in the dry southwest, but this bird is unusual for its ability to go without drinking water for days at a time. (Charlie Ott)

will catch on the wing, darting out from a bush or tree. In California this bird nests in the desert early in the year and then migrates to a wetter area where it breeds again. Most of the birds do not migrate regularly but travel about in search of berries within their range.

BLACK-THROATED SPARROW

We have already met another member of the finch family, the evening grosbeak, in the chapter on forest birds, but this bird is much smaller and is particularly adapted to life in the desert. Like many finches, it has a strong bill (though not as large as the grosbeak's) and feeds on insects and seeds, which it picks up from the ground, along with enough gravel to enable the gizzard to digest its food. Apparently, the black-throated sparrow takes in enough moisture in its food to allow it to go without water during the driest part of the desert year; in fact, it seems to prefer the hottest weather and can be found even in Death Valley, which is inhospitable to so much plant and animal life.

The cactus wren, as its name implies, builds its nest in a cactus, and it also feeds on the cactus fruit and berries. Like the plant it is found in the southwestern deserts.
(G. C. Kelley)

BIRDS OF THE MOUNTAINS

Like the desert, the mountains of western North America offer a demanding habitat. There are extremes of temperature, heavy snows, and strong winds, but what makes the mountains so inaccessible to humans—the dense coniferous forests and the dramatically shifting landscape—is just what makes them appealing to many birds, whose flying abilities enable them to get around very easily indeed where many other animals cannot. The evergreen trees provide good shelter and a rich variety of vegetation, which in turn supports a wealth of insect life, offering mountain birds excellent feeding opportunities.

MOUNTAIN QUAIL

In spite of the rough mountain terrain, this large, hand-

The golden eagle (above) lives in mountains all over the world—Asia, North Africa, Europe, and North America. It is a powerful and graceful flier and is more abundant than the bald eagle (left), although there are estimated to be only a few thousand pairs left on our continent. (Tom McHugh, above; Phyllis Greenberg, left)

some member of the pheasant family is a ground bird like its cousins, living in dense underbrush and in open areas of the forest, nesting on the ground beneath the trees and hiding itself when disturbed, since its coloration provides a good camouflage. This bird can fly if necessary but prefers to travel on foot; it can run at more than ten miles per hour and often moves on foot down the mountains in the fall as far as forty or fifty miles. The mountain quail has a varied diet—leaves and flowers or other vegetation in the warmer months, as well as some insects, seeds, and fruits during the rest of the year as they are available.

BLACK SWIFT

Although this bird lives in much of the same range as the mountain quail, its existence is very different indeed, since it spends most of its time in the air. The swift family is very well named, for these birds are capable of the swiftest flight of any small bird (their legs are so weak, however, that they

The mountain quail, which lives in the mountain ranges of the west, is the largest and most attractive quail in North America. (Bill Reasons; see page 85.)

Swifts are among the best fliers of all birds and seem to spend all their lives in the air, feeding, drinking, courting, and bathing on the wing. Three of the four North American swifts are found in the mountains of the west, where the difficult terrain offers little challenge. The chimney swift is also found in the east, where it has adapted to human terrain, nesting in barns, chimneys, and silos rather than on cliffs. (Steve Maslowski)

have difficulty taking off from land). The alpine swift, a European species that feeds on the wing like the black swift of North America, has been clocked at eighty miles per hour.

Swifts have streamlined bodies with long, pointed wings and short or forked tails and have sharp claws that they use to cling to cliffs and walls (as does the chimney swift, which often nests in manmade buildings). The black swift flies high over the mountains and builds its nest on cliffs or ledges, often flying far from home during the nesting season and migrating to tropical areas during the winter. Although this is the largest of the swifts it is not often seen by man and is presumed rare. Another name for the bird is cloud swift, since it will follow rainclouds for miles feeding in the insect-rich air.

COPPERY-TAILED TROGON

This is a tropical bird that has somehow managed to adapt to a life in the canyons of the mountains of southern Arizona as well as points south. It is an attractive bird of glossy green or bronze, with bright-red chest and white markings and a long tail, but it is not nearly so spectacular as its cousin the resplendant quetzal of Central America, which was regarded as sacred by the Aztecs. Although the trogon eats fruit and berries, it prefers insects, picking them off leaves while it hovers in the air. It builds its nest in tree holes abandoned by woodpeckers or occurring naturally in sycamores and lives alone or in pairs, making a rather raucous cry; like the peacock, it is perhaps better seen than heard.

MOUNTAIN BLUEBIRD

This lovely bird is one of the thrush family, which also includes the American robin and the eastern and western bluebirds. This species can be distinguished from the other bluebirds because the male has no reddish coloring on its breast but is almost entirely blue; the female is a faded brown in color with a bit of blue on her tail. Like its cousins, the mountain bluebird feeds mostly on insects, with occasional berries when they are in season, and it too is a fine singer, the male warbling to its mate during the breeding season. Unfortunately, this bird is rare and conservationists are concerned about its status. Although the robin and the other bluebirds are familiar to most Americans, this bird is uncommon and is restricted in range to the mountains of the northwest, wintering farther south into Mexico, Texas, and several midwestern states. Its eggs are pale blue, similar to those of the robin and several of the other thrushes.

WESTERN TANAGER

This bird, which is native to the Rocky Mountains, was first discovered by Lewis and Clark. It is a member of the tanager family, which includes many brilliantly colored birds, such as the scarlet tanager, a familiar sight throughout much of North America. Unlike that bird, which prefers deciduous forests, the western tanager summers in the coniferous forests of the west up to ten thousand feet, building its nest high off the ground on the branches of pines, firs, and other trees. The tanager feeds primarily on insects, including wasps and termites, and on berries and other kinds of fruit. The female incubates the eggs for two weeks, but the male helps her feed the babies. After the nesting season, the birds fly south to Mexico or Costa Rica to spend the colder months.

GOLDEN EAGLE

The mountains of the American west are impressive indeed, and the most impressive bird of that region is unquestionably the golden eagle, a member of the hawk family. With a wingspread of six to seven and a half feet, this bird is one of nature's best fliers, moving its wings slowly in powerful strokes and gliding or soaring on thermals often for hours at a time, reaching great heights, and capable of diving toward earth at speeds of up to two hundred miles per hour. Like other birds of prey, the eagle feeds on small animals—rodents, snakes, birds, and insects—but because of its size, this bird can, if necessary, take much larger prey, such as full-grown deer and sheep, though it usually does not attack healthy animals of this size.

These birds generally have a large territory, thirty or more square miles, in which they can hunt without competition and raise their young, who may depend on their

The male western tanager is one of the most colorful birds in the Rockies, where it nests high above the ground at the end of tree branches. (Allan D. Cruickshank)

The mountain bluebird is well named, living in mountain meadows of the west often as high as ten thousand feet above sea level. (Anthony Mercieca)

parents for three months or more after hatching. They prefer to make their enormous nests, which can be ten feet across, on cliffs overlooking their hunting ground, and they often use the nests for generations, though they will also build alternative nests and use them in rotation year after year. Sheepherders once killed great numbers of these birds, which are now fully protected by law, because it was thought, erroneously, that they preyed heavily on livestock, but this has been proved not to be the case, since their primary diet is rabbits. Like other hawks, the golden eagle is long-lived, often living thirty years or more, even in the wild.

CALIFORNIA CONDOR

Vultures are closely related to hawks and falcons, and all three families are in the same order, Falconiformes, but unlike the other groups, vultures feed almost entirely on carrion. In fact, there is no evidence that a California condor has ever killed a living animal, preferring instead to circle around in the air watching for large animals that have already died. They are not handsome birds, having featherless heads and necks (perhaps this helps them avoid contamination when they eat decayed meat), and their feet are not as sharp as those of the hawks and falcons, since they do not have to seize and hold their prey. They are, however, graceful fliers, with the largest wingspread of any American bird at up to nine and a half feet, and they spend much of their time in the air soaring and watching for food with their extremely keen eyes. They do not build nests but simply lay their eggs on bare cliffs; incubation may take as long as fifty days, and the chick (there is only one for the California condor) may be fed by the parents for as long as a year. Condors can live for many years, well beyond thirty, but few last so long in the wild.

Although the feeding habits of the condor and the other vultures are extremely useful in nature, helping to clean up decaying matter, they are often shot by hunters and ranchers and may be killed by feeding on coyotes that have been poisoned by ranchers. In spite of its remote range in the mountains of California, the slow birth rate and human interference have caused this bird to become one of the rarest in the world, and it is unlikely that the California condor will survive as a species into the twenty-first century. There are fewer than twenty birds alive today, and though efforts to save the birds have been undertaken, causing the bird to become for many the symbol of conservation, this noble creature, once called the thunderbird by Indians, is likely to join the passenger pigeon, the Carolina parakeet, and the great auk in the list of species made extinct by the behavior of the human race.

The coppery-tailed trogon is a Central American bird that also nests in the mountains of southern Arizona. (Tom McHugh; see page 86.)

The California condor is undoubtedly the rarest North American bird. Heroic efforts are now being made to save the species from extinction. (Kenneth W. Fink)

STATE BIRDS

Alabama	Yellow-shafted flicker	Montana	Western meadowlark
Alaska	Willow ptarmigan	Nebraska	Western meadowlark
Arizona	Cactus wren	Nevada	Mountain bluebird
Arkansas	Mockingbird	New Hampshire	Purple finch
California	California quail	New Jersey	American goldfinch
Colorado	Lark bunting	New Mexico	Roadrunner
Connecticut	American robin	New York	Eastern bluebird
Delaware	Blue hen chicken	North Carolina	Cardinal
District of Columbia	Wood thrush	North Dakota	Western meadowlark
Florida	Mockingbird	Ohio	Cardinal
Georgia	Brown thrasher	Oklahoma	Scissor-tailed flycatcher
Hawaii	Hawaiian goose	Oregon	Western meadowlark
Idaho	Mountain bluebird	Pennsylvania	Ruffed grouse
Illinois	Cardinal	Rhode Island	Rhode Island red (chicken)
Indiana	Cardinal	South Carolina	Carolina wren
Iowa	American goldfinch	South Dakota	Ring-necked pheasant
Kansas	Western meadowlark	Tennessee	Mockingbird
Kentucky	Cardinal	Texas	Mockingbird
Louisiana	Brown pelican	Utah	California gull
Maine	Black-capped chickadee	Vermont	Hermit thrush
Maryland	Baltimore (northern) oriole	Virginia	Cardinal
Massachusetts	Black-capped chickadee	Washington	Willow goldfinch
Michigan	American robin	West Virginia	Cardinal
Minnesota	Common loon	Wisconsin	American robin
Mississippi	Mockingbird	Wyoming	Western meadowlark
Missouri	Eastern bluebird		

SUGGESTED READING

There are many books about the birds of North America, of which we can list only a few for the interested reader who wishes to explore the subject further. One of the most popular illustrated books is John James Audubon's *Birds of America*, originally published in 1870 and now available in a number of editions, both costly and inexpensive. The most comprehensive field guides are those by Roger Tory Peterson; his *Field Guide to the Birds (Eastern Land and Water Birds)* and *Field Guide to Western Birds* (both, Houghton Mifflin) have recently been revised and are the standard books for field identification; they are illustrated with drawings and paintings by the author. The *Audubon Society Field Guide to North American Birds*, available in two volumes (one for eastern species, one for western) and pub-

lished by Alfred A. Knopf, are also excellent, illustrated with photographs in full color as well as maps and sketches. The Golden Press book entitled *Birds of North America*, by Robbins, Bruun, and Zim, is a good general introduction, and *The Audubon Society Encyclopedia of North American Birds* by John K. Terres, with over sixteen hundred illustrations, many of them in color, and nearly six thousand entries, is certainly the most comprehensive volume available to the general reader (Knopf). Roger F. Pasquier's *Watching Birds: An Introduction to Ornithology* (Houghton Mifflin) is not a guide to species but an excellent discussion of various different aspects of bird life and gives much helpful and insightful advice to the bird-watcher.

INDEX OF BIRDS